ASTONISHMENTS

Tasha Cotter

FUTURECYCLE PRESS
www.futurecycle.org

Cover photo, "Pigeon Mosaic" by Bikansky; author photo by Sarah Caton; cover and interior book design by Diane Kistner; Adobe Garamond Pro text and Paddington SC titling

Library of Congress Control Number: 2019957975

Published by FutureCycle Press
Athens, Georgia, USA

ISBN 978-1-942371-96-0

To my family

CONTENTS

"Some things you cannot forget: furrows in your memory, packed and preserved with snow."

—Sarah Gorham
Alpine Apprentice

"…you will find me, God,
Like a dumb pigeon's beak I am
Pecking
My way at astonishment."

—Ilya Kaminsky
"A Cigarette"

WOKE

At first, I didn't feel anything,
Face to face with the dogwood tree,
A giant swirl of mint and youth.
Its thousand eyes saw every bit
Of me, alone and undisguised.
But what surprised me most
Was how it stood its ground,
Insisting I respect its shapely
Drama. It was then I realized
I'd been waiting out a feeling
Of catastrophe, a sadness
That loops around, unwilling
To let me out. Roots wrestle
The ground. It's an ancient war,
Becoming who you are: one minute
A burst of knowing, the next
A burrowing in. The mystery
Was hiding. The tree was alive
When I wasn't sure how to be.
Then, I knew I had to keep going—
Maybe there was still beauty like life
That hides, then appears and thrives.

WHITE ROSES

After the storm, the flowers
Lay weakened, some badly
Broken clean off the stalk.
I walked through the rose garden
And counted five hundred or so
Miniature heads strewn across
The ground. Their whitened,
Curled petals reminded me
Of an ancient war I once read
About, how the Vikings pillaged
The Irish countryside, throwing
Babies onto swords. What must
It have been like to see the ship
Approaching the shore? To turn
Their strange voices and shouts
Over in one's head like a stone?
I've seen the roots of violence
Burrow and tug in some hearts,
But I've not watched my life
Start to slip away as men sing
Their foreign song into the wind
Of my ear. I've not seen my young
Butchered. I wanted to write you
Something pretty among the roses,
But these ruddy bouquets want
Me to tell you about how war begins
With a slow anchoring in. We sense
What's coming before it pierces us
Like thorns. I'm telling you there are
Stories much worse than you or I

Will ever know, and this truth leaves
Me cold, searching the rose garden
For some trace of beauty, but the clouds
Are darkening and the roses lie quietly
As if waiting out a raid among
The withered, bloodied, and red.

DREAMING RED

In the middle of your life, a cave
Of terrible things no one bothered to explain
To you when you were a child, how you came from
Blood and gunshot, how they worried over
Your adolescent heartbreak, fearing the same
Tortured end. There are some terrors you don't
Have to be told, the twin ghosts of what you suspect
And what you know haunt your dreams, taunting
You with their half-smiles. Desire and its chariot
Of horses visit me in darkness and a parade
Of sparklers break their white-hot heat in my chest.
I wonder if this feeling is anything like
The last days of my great-grandparents—the double
Suicide. His last half-smile before he shot himself
After she found someone else. She didn't survive
That inheritance of loss. Time spirals
Silently on, a twisting knife through the years.
What's left? The person finding the body, carefully
Seeing what's left of her white neck, her winning smile.

SOLAR

For mom

Disregard the glittering iced coffees, bought on the golden chain
    highway.
The world, back then, was hot. A hundred degrees by mid-afternoon.
    You locked the pool. Locked the door. Took a wrong turn
Toward Oakhurst and circled back. Pointed out the mule deer
    Eating what remained of the Nevada blue-eyed grass in what remained
Of California in its four-year drought. Tuesday was Half Dome.
    Wednesday was Mariposa Grove where a circle of Sequoias
Stood in prayer deep in the sanctuary of Yosemite. *This is the last thing*
    We'll ever do together, you said. And so I defied the bucking yellow-
Tinged landscape. Braved the white-hot mesas and blistering heat.
    We stood at Glacier Point, Curry Village at our feet.
I was thinking about the solar panels on the property, arranged
    In careful tiers, the occasional square spectrum of black nests
On the ranch. How at first I didn't know what I'd been looking at.
    I saw them and then I stopped seeing them. Days passed.
I thought they were bleachers. *That's what powers this place,* you said.
    The sunlight feeds the place we've been living in.
We stood there, our heads drifting to the blood-orange horizon.
    I want to be back on the light buff granite, staring down the side
    of a mountain.

Vow

The doves find a spot
Of shade under a bench
And sit together, quietly
Speaking about the world
Of people and rain. They recall
The dog they once saw,
How they had nightmares
For weeks. They agree
The clouds are moving
Faster today, more blue
Than gray. How soft
The sky looks—almost
Delicate—like a cursive
Letter of love was written
And finger-stirred, thickly
Left to light and diffuse the sky.

THREE VARIATIONS

I.

A littered desk, the afternoon
Snack, the apple left a small pool of moisture.
Core upturned, remaining on the desk.

II.

There's a park that's not really
A park where I can go, alone,
And wait for evening—or nothing.

III.

Some days the time feels like enough
Time. It's not flying. It's just moving
The same way I do: ordered, unnoticed.

THE SOUNDING BIRD

Tonight, I heard it—
The evening chirp

Of our sounding bird
Dressed in colors

Of rust and autumn.
She's spent her life

In love, among the trees.
She doesn't think

Of future beasts
Or wild things.

Her heart, the perfect
Shelter. A little seed.

Surely a sigh must
Quietly leave her

To see him waiting,
Evening, beginning.

THE PATIENT

I've learned the trick is to not watch
The needle. I let her dab the crook
Of my arm with a wet piece of white
Cotton, a cold press of alcohol
Before the needle goes in. I wonder
What my blood will tell her this time.
The place is closing up. I'm the last
Patient. I'm ready to be stung
By the cool touch of the needle;
For my body to be woken up.
I need it to remember certain things.
We make small talk about Easter,
And I try to channel my mother;
A lion-tamer of pain, she could
Carry on whole conversations this way.
I wondered if she, too, spent her life
Always praying for the same thing.

THE GYNECOLOGIST

When he found out
I was going to France
For three months
The summer after
My junior year, he
Said I should have
No trouble being
Confused for an
American. I dressed
So nicely. So…
European, he said,
And the moment
Shifted into something
Else. His kindness
Layered between
Two things I couldn't
Name or didn't want
To say. To this day
It's not foreign men
I worry about. It's
The men I know
Well. The ones who
Linger a little too
Long on the sound
Of my name.

SILENCE

The deer must have known
I ached for a friend.
There's a kind of famine
That comes in autumn—
The afternoon half-light
That allows you to see
Clearly for miles and yet
You won't see the deer
And you won't have that
Gladness. You won't see
What's there, there.

November

I remember what it was like, the last time.
I know the season, the twist of the air,
And what happened that winter. How broken
We all were. How we lugged our new
Sorrows across your white, snowy world
Of time. Winter took hold of my life.
I learned a girl can get buried before it's
Her time. I'd sit in my truck waiting for you
To break the ice in the predawn cold.
There was nowhere else I could go, and so
I froze in that foreign land, caught between
The two of them, and that winter was all
Whisper. Lost, I began to forget who I was
And who I'd been. A daughter forced to tear
Through the ugliness that lets itself out
On all of us. I thought I was done becoming
Who I was, but I wasn't done with the hurt
And hurting people. Turns out, no one was.

MOTHER SPEAKS OF LEAVES

I left them for too long. Now the leaves
Cover everything. And they're not even ugly,
No, seeing them all like this—a golden
Carpet, really, the tans and oranges, but look
At how they cover everything now—
How they've wedged themselves in the hostas;
Now the green grass is covered by leaves.
Even the walkway—yes, can you see it?—
You can barely make out the path now.
It's hard to see the path—hidden by leaves!

LOVE POEM

Entering the museum, we followed signs in the low light
    To the gems and minerals room. Inside,
All manner of mined and dug up earth was on display: the sharp glint
       of tetrahedra,
    Quartz catching a flash of light. In the room of rare things,
Trophy rubies and sapphires. Thousands of stones
    Were carefully positioned behind the glass,
Silently waiting in their private enchantment. Lost in a giant sea
    Of astonishment, I remembered my old love of fool's
Gold. The cool touch of mineral, the slick eyes of topaz. I've learned
    That everything is a result of various forms of chemistry.
For example, diamonds are the hardest natural material,
    And yet I couldn't take my eyes away from the black night
of Galena: the exhibit of coal-dark mineral, stacked like a sculpture
    Of shiny cubed ice, space-like in its depth. It's not that native gold
Wasn't there, but it was the amber that reminded me of you—there, near
       the end—
    As the black path grew lit with yellow drops of golden romance,
A hush of brilliance softly pieced me back together, heavy with memory,
       born again.

THE INHERITANCE

I've learned history can sink
Hard into earth, yet water runs

And hides. I am your daughter,

Bedeviled shadow; keeper
Of your five remaining school

Pictures. They say I'm the twin
Of my mother. The speed-

Walker of fields, intent
On doing it all. I don't know

Where this need comes from.
I collect the stones of resemblance:

The careful speech of farm

Animals, tenderhearted, hard
To get to know. I observe

The many forms of busyness

That borders on running away.
I'm told to love in a way that dodges

And deflects the most-prized
Things most others will say.

HOW NOT TO EAT A LOBSTER

Rockport, Massachusetts

It helps to not look at the tank to the right,
    Filled with their green and brown bodies, banded
And stacked several inches high. No, stick to the line,
    Taking one step forward each time
The person in front of you moves aside. "Two for the deck"
    Buys you two lobsters, each curled
In a white box. Corpse-like and steamed to a bright red,
    Their bodies just cool enough to touch.
A tiny tub of liquefied butter pressed gently beside the right eye.
    If you want to eat a lobster, it's better not to think
Of this as a burial or to consider in what world
    A funeral instructs its guests to squeeze and crack
The deceased before dunking the body in a plastic bowl of fat. No,
    It was the tail fan that gave me pause; how able
It must have been, casting around on the Atlantic floor, maneuvering
    Over every rock, searching for mollusks. It must have felt
Something like satisfaction at catching lunch. It must have been
    Content with its life burrowing in crevices and stone, deep
In watery silence, living in the easy darkness of the only life it knew.

How She Appears

In the window—cold and rushed, royal
As so many need her. Then, the left vapor
Of a departed ghost. The room empties.
They'll wait quietly for her as they always do.
Her voice leaves a trail of strange pleasure:
Laughter. The shadowy blue fabric sweeps
At the rise and fall of her knees; the silk
Outlines her arms, discreetly, as smoke
In winter rises in the distance. She turns
Once to see herself fading into what's
There: the apparition glistens, assessing her.
Is she missing if she disappears into what's left?

Family Time

My father always had a dash of the pragmatist:
Of broken, hurting animals, he'd matter-of-factly say
It was the circle of life (without a smile on his face).
My mother would sometimes complain that we never had
Any family time. He worked Monday through Friday.
Worked Saturdays, too. On Sundays we'd wake and get ready
For church and by the time we got home, it was time
For lunch. He was always in a rush to get back to work
On his or his father's farm. Years later,
Divorced and alone, I watched him stare out the living
Room window, distant, his voice slow and considered.
I suspected he might say something about regrets, tell me
Who he was for once and for all, but he ever
So gently confessed that he finally liked the look of the land.

CONFESSION

No one tells you there will always be
The list of things you can admit to—
The unfortunate thing you said
At rush hour in the direction
Of the other driver, or the mess
You made of your last relationship.
I sometimes dream about leaving
You, but the dream always ends before
I see where I go, as if somehow I sense
The impossibility of the rest. What's left
Is the guilt of what I did and didn't do.
There are some things I can't admit.
The difficult, the unrecognizable.
Let it stay buried under the weight
Of time, unspeakable. Hidden, tortured.

Cape Ann, Summer

He'd just sat up to watch the waves when he noticed the family arriving on the beach, not twenty feet away. A mother and father with their young son, who was just learning to walk, toddled between both of them, tentative, laughing. The man watched the mother, softly smiling, their soft voices carried a little on the breeze. He couldn't make out the words, only the tone of happiness, the feeling of a good memory being made. How sweet it all looked, and how reasonably she took to motherhood. He could feel the heat of the sun on his back,; his cheeks were turning pink in the broad afternoon light. His eyes landed on their little bag of beach toys, and he admired the soundness of the scene. He lay back down beside her, considering them, considering his own mistake.

AN ANNOUNCEMENT OF PRIZES

To the farmhouse that stood waiting for me at the end of Wolf Pen road,
a step onto your gravel driveway. A carpeting of yellowed leaves.

To the sun setting over the county line, delivering us soon, to winter,
an empty coffee mug scrubbed with the damp sponge.

To the man I was told to contact should I want to walk around this
property in bow-season, an empty bench, cold to touch.

To the afternoon wren that darted into my bedroom window and rose again
to your branch, this poem, this wing of hope.

To the wasps endlessly walking and tracking their steps along the glass,
a secret pocket, a guide of air.

To the buckling cracks and rotted window panes, a pair of eyes that
won't see the brokenness of your hips, sees only a family of lights dotting
the hillside.

A MARRIAGE

One day you will surely get tired
Of the checklists and monotonous tasks.
You'll get tired of me, too, and all
The colorful collars I put on you.
You, who would rather stay in and read
In bed. You, maker of ham and biscuits
Served with molasses. Marriage is
A hologram capturing the interference
Of our scattered light. Michelangelo
Destroyed most of his drawings before
He died, not wanting others to see
How difficult it had been for him,
The slow work of getting good. The work
Is easy, some days, even freeing. Yet some
Weeks I can't get it right, and neither can
You. Together we fail the simple test
Of each other's happiness, but it's what we love:
This holy work; this invention of us.

AFTER

The spectacle and swarm, the arms loose, body
Torn, I imagine he went inside the praetorium

To a lunch of oily fish—sardines, perhaps
A loaf of bread, plated with olives,—collapsed

Into his seat in a room of white marble, thinking
Through the morning. Glad to be released

From the mob of high priests. Procula
Glances at him and says nothing. He was told

Of her dream. The visitation and warning—
Her servant raced to him, mid-trial, to warn him

Of this man. And now, his lips slick with oil,
He notices an eclipse forming; the standards

Fall from the walls. Procula jumps from her chair.
The ground begins to tremble underfoot. His release:

A scream and shout as a wave of Judeans rush
Out of their houses, distressed

About what it meant. Pilate knew only the death
Of certain men are met with an anger like this. A hint

Of terror sweeps through him; a rush of thunder rattles
The darkened sky as his soldiers glance his way,

Searching for a sign as their fates swirl and darken around them.

35

I write your name in my familiar way:
In silver ink, all uppercase, in the middle of the page.
The card now waits for your 35th birthday.
What better way, I wanted to say, of getting older—
Than what? Somewhere in the alleyways
Of my brain, I lost what I wanted
To tell you, fumbling the message. It was
Something about how to celebrate,
Or how we must surely be better
Than we were. The concert I bought you tickets for
Will be a band you recognize (one form of lightness)
That arrived around the same time I did.
I bought my first bottle of wine the night
Of our first meal together, having just turned
Twenty-one. I got lost in the aisles of reds and whites,
And so we've been celebrating since the day we met.
I love this quiet party—I don't miss the rest. The years
Spool out from the beginning. What I meant to tell you
Is it's true, you're getting older and what better way.

THE COUPLE

I want to discover them
All over again, selling mums
In the roadside garden,
Her trying to decide between
Fried chicken or beef
Stroganoff for lunch, him
Doing the odd jobs that had
To get done. Now, the look
Of confusion as ideas get lost
On the long passageways
Of thought. I say it's easy
To forget names and to mistake
Things. Time is a thief,
Robbing us in our sleep.
What's left? A heap of belongings,
Cuckoo clocks and porcelain
Teacups. Their voices soften;
Personality flattens. The air
Briefly spasms in bursts
Of liveliness, then swaths of quiet.
I imagine life was a movie once—
In which they did everything. But the way
She quietly takes her place now
In her dining room—on her stage—
I wait. There's nothing left to say.

POEM ON OUR TEN-YEAR WEDDING ANNIVERSARY

I'll never write to you
Like I wrote to you.
Still—this arc of heaven
We've found: so surprising
To see it's made of stone
And fool's gold, carefully
Woven like a crown.

Trapani

She remembered the day had felt endless and now night was coming, too. Where would they stay? They knew nothing about Trapani. This was in 2007 and they'd taken a bus there on their honeymoon to Calampiso. They'd kept walking the streets and wondering if they'd find some place to spend the night. Then, late that evening, they checked into a place. It was nearly 1 a.m. when she heard the lock on their door turn. She froze, then whispered to him—*Is someone at the door?* He got up and turned on the light. She was terrified. She remembers waiting for her life to change. What was going to happen to them? But whatever had been there left. The next day, when she asked him about what they'd heard, he didn't remember anything. The way he looked at her, like she made it all up.

COUNTRY WALKS

"I've often wondered
What the fence keeps out
In a country bereft of predators."

—Steven Toussaint, "Agnes Dei"

The country walk
Was not something
You saw.

Instead, the carved
Land, partitioned off.

I spent a long time
Wondering at the sense
Of being locked out—

Of what?

When all around me
Space stretched out,
Overwhelming
In its endlessness,

Broken up by electrical
Hot wires. Neon plastic.
Banks of fence.

No one could wonder
At their freedom.

Weren't we free

Inside with our windows,
Feeling we were
Just shy of trespassers?

WHAT WILL SURELY HAPPEN

The fact is I will lose my mother,
And the mere possibility breaks me,
Cooling the blood in my chest. Sometimes
The slow-motion terror of it all quiets
Everything else until my heart snaps
Back. Not that she will leave me
Anytime soon, but she will, won't she?
The woman who taught me to help others
And how to take orders with a smile.
She opened herself up to the world
Generously. I was never very good
At that. We talk nightly, me and my
Mother. Last week she had pneumonia,
But it was me who was scared to death.
When she lost five pounds, she joked
About the weight loss, told me she was going
To buy a new dress to wear around town.
Now, when we hang up with each other,
A part of me—the part that's my mother?—
Says *honey, it'll come. Life is coming*
For you. You've got to grow up. Life is
Going to break you—and I mean break you—
Some more.

A Room Full of People

For Andrew Coffey

When he died alone
In a room full of people,

Some playing pool,
Drinking, and partying
At the fraternity,

Did he at least feel
The glittering I had felt, too,
When I was twenty?

Or did it just feel sour,
A constant wave of panic

And rage. No one tried to help him,
Not right away. They waited

And then it was too late.
There's a sameness
I don't like to think about:

I was there in the same kind
Of place, as a girl. Just
A particle, too, in that haze.

Would anyone have noticed
If I'd slipped away with you?

No Poem Will Ever Be Good Enough

For the geese who arrived that night,
Descending at dusk. I'd arrived
At my father's house; you could call
It my childhood home, but, now, different.
I'd stepped outside that December night
And caught them descending just like
I remembered them—flying in
From the other side, going from one
Pond to another. Who knows,
Maybe they learned the flight path
From their mother. I wanted to stand
Outside a little longer, despite the cold,
Remembering my old life—how familiar
It had been. But now? I was some place
Else. Standing in a house, not a home.

OLD PICTURES

She placed the box in front of us
That December, after lunch. In it,
Old pictures, many black and white;
The others in faded colors, square
Portraits with thin white borders. Pictures
Of her homeplace: Hyden and Hazard
And, later, Winchester where they had
The orchard. There were pictures of sisters
That had been. Families of ten, eleven
People. I studied them, memorizing
The tailored dresses and three-piece suits.
The rail-thin men stood alongside
The proud women who rarely smiled.
It makes you realize how few things
Stick around: a single picture exists
Of your great-grandparents' fiftieth
Wedding anniversary. Just a single
Black and white print of them at a picnic
Table—a lunch of soup beans, corn bread,
And greens spread in front of them. Then
Comes the sixtieth wedding anniversary
Picture, this one in color, the platters
A little bigger. I shift the pictures to you
Across the table, wondering at these lives
Left for us to decipher. We, too, will
Someday appear distant and quaint. How
Many times will someone repeat our names—
And who will be the "they" clutching
Each picture, knowing time will take them, too.

THE YEARS

Sitting alone in an unknown room,
Time shuts a door you didn't know
Was there. Candles quicken
In the windows; memories flame
Up, abate. The days, unadorned,
Are poured into us like hushed lakes.

THE WOODS

To this day, I can't say what came between them.
I suspect it may have been a farm they acquired,
The one that was mostly forest. For once,
She loved a piece of land as much as him.
It was a source of pride for both of them,
Owning a piece of unspoiled woods, and they
Each dreamed of the rabbits, wolves, and birds
Who lived there, and loved it, too. And so, when
He sold the woods for timber, the land cleared
Without her knowledge, she turned against him
For taking a rare thing and selling it off like it was
Nothing. For destroying so many shelters, whose
Voices she could hear; whose, she feared, he couldn't.

TURTLES

The clay mud was stuck to us for weeks
After the pond draining. You'd find specks
Behind your ears, bits of dirt attached
To your back. So many people came out
That day. The preacher's children and I
Played hide-and-seek, improvised slides
In the excavated streams as the pond drained
Into the field. We slid down the muddy waves,
Leapt off the dock, lunched on hot dogs.
At sunset I watched the last of the turtles
Cross the marsh. The purity of that pleasure
Is what I miss: before I could question him
About spilling what was filled. I could
Stand knee-deep in skeletons, rot, and decay
And ride the clay water-slides the machine made.
Even as the sun set, I didn't understand the end.
I never questioned why he'd change anything.

Men at Work

In the summer, the navy shirt
Of my father was more veneer
Than anything real. The fabric
Worn thin, I'd marvel at the way
Cotton darkened and fastened itself
To him. When evening came, you knew
He'd given everything. His speech
Labored and weak, salt ash swept
Along the bank of his neck. In July
The white dust coated him,
Muting his rust-colored skin. Now
No one I know looks like he did
At the end of the day. I know what
My father would say—something
About men not being real men—then go
Quiet, considering what's changed.

THE RISING DARK

Propped against the kitchen cabinet,
She waits as he mans the spatula,
The slow morning burning off them.
A war of nothing fills the air.
She watches the way he reminds her
Of himself only yesterday doing
The same thing: a small motion
Of the wrist and their eggs flip
As one in the pan; they sizzle
And pop. She knows he's looking
For a signal as if what's done is done;
Where is the cue they have lost?
She wonders what he is waiting for.
The scent of burning as they stare
And stare. For better or for worse,
She can't remember this turn.

FAMILIAR

We know how it ends:

With lace—with hands.
The day ends the same way

The decades began. Slow
Gasps of the machine

Left wheezing in the corner.

No one comes closer;
I imagine the air twirls

And lifts

Like it always did. Curls
Up and falls—heavy

Upon the quilt. Rest
(If you prefer, *death*)

Walks up to you like a cat.

It settles in and sinks
Heavy on your chest:

Glad to have found you
To claim you, like this—

INCARNADINE

The word a color of flesh— a tongue,
Rough skin, the inside of your cheek.
We've all dreamed in those shades
Of red and pain. *Wake up—you were
Calling out in your sleep.* The soft tissue
Around the cherry pit. A slick of clear
Pink. The fingers we lick. Did we know
That pain had a name? Lips, ochre, and pale
Burning. We love but the love is rusting.

MARCH ROBIN

Incredibly, no one
    Else is stopping
To admire the perfect
    Heft of her copper-
Colored chest.

THE LIVING

Say the loss may never be credible;
How it taunts us, lying there, about to fall
Off the table.

The surgical way it all happens: a cut
Here and soon the wound is sewn.

You feel the little stone inside, the little
Stitch in one side. You are not as you were.

You will confront the ending and its shades
Of meaning. At a certain time of day
The light is especially bright.

You keep track of the light, when it shines brightest.

You go on living and life dwarfs the worst part.
You go on living and noise cancels out that one part.

Sometimes, she'll call me when she's seen
His new wife, and there's nothing I can do.

I want to say *you were bound to run
Into that one part....*

And life carries on greenly, lit by the sun,
And the one flower at a distance blooms red
As it curves against a wall of white-hot wind.

THE PRESENT EVERYTHING

Most of the time we have no idea how time will change us.

For a year I asked God to make me better. To make me
Good, loving, patient, *helpful to others,* even. I asked
And then forgot what I asked for.

On the first day of spring I stepped outside to find one
Snake; then, an hour later, another had joined the first
Snake. By the end of the day three snakes—

At the end of my terror, I didn't mind. When I followed
My panic down its steel tunnel, I didn't mind.

I clean and purge, watch the gray-cream of my walls
Grow half a shade whiter; the smooth gloss of water rinses
The dust and pet hair and scorched oil from wood.

I know an old woman who shops for groceries. She doesn't
Cook or clean but keeps collecting the present everything:
Papers, napkins, canned goods, and consignment shirts.

Because there is no room for any of it, she stacks it all
As carefully as she can. Her life is a tyranny of the past:
Paper bags of old mail, paper cups, and nylon bags

She can't get rid of. She is lost somewhere in the panic
Tunnel. I want to know what the swamp looked like
As she saw the black water rise, the aloneness creep in

And infect her bones. The boat, breaking. In the distance
More emptiness even as she called and called.

THE FUTURE

I should want more than to stare into this valley,
Thinking about the nothing of my body. In the future,
I already know the expression I'll wear: the woman
Who was always a girl going to war. It will be like
It always was: I'll wear things you won't like.
I'll still be reading about monsters in my free time.
I let the people I love disappear. I see myself in the slow
Becoming. I'm a hope chest of distressing things
And everybody's watching or I'm invisible.
Not broken. Not naive. Still, the world won't let go
Of me. My mother tells me five people asked
Her if I was pregnant yet last week, and I'm angry
With everyone for finding the failure. For burying my nose in it.
For confiscating my fistful of happiness and sending
Me into the air, spent, like the arrows of a dandelion. What is
This? This is me trying to say I'm brave, and I'm afraid
My future doesn't matter. I'm afraid it will be lonely
Forever listening to their whispers of *how disappointing.*

ACKNOWLEDGEMENTS

Thanks to the editors from the following publications in which some of these poems previously appeared:

Thrush Poetry Journal: "Silence"
River's Edge: "Woke"
New Limestone Review: "The Patient," "Love Poem"
The Write Launch: "Vow," "Three Variations," "November"
Superstition Review: "Solar"
LEO Weekly: "White Roses"

Thanks to the Kentucky Foundation for Women for an Artist Enrichment grant in 2018, which helped support the creation of some of these poems.

The poem "Solar" was included in *Fire and Rain: Ecopoetry of California* (Scarlet Tanager Books, 2018).

ACKNOWLEDGMENTS

ABOUT FUTURECYCLE PRESS

FutureCycle Press is dedicated to publishing lasting English-language poetry books, chapbooks, and anthologies in both print-on-demand and Kindle ebook formats. Founded in 2007 by independent editor/publishers and partners Diane Kistner and Robert S. King, the press incorporated as a nonprofit in 2012. A number of our editors are distinguished poets and writers in their own right, and we have been actively involved in the small press movement going back to the early seventies.

The FutureCycle Poetry Book Prize and honorarium is awarded annually for the best full-length volume of poetry we publish in a calendar year. Introduced in 2013, our Good Works projects are anthologies devoted to issues of universal significance, with all proceeds donated to a related worthy cause. Our Selected Poems series highlights contemporary poets with a substantial body of work to their credit; with this series we strive to resurrect work that has had limited distribution and is now out of print.

We are dedicated to giving all of the authors we publish the care their work deserves, making our catalog of titles the most diverse and distinguished it can be, and paying forward any earnings to fund more great books.

We've learned a few things about independent publishing over the years. We've also evolved a unique, resilient publishing model that allows us to focus mainly on vetting and preserving for posterity poetry collections of exceptional quality without becoming overwhelmed with bookkeeping and mailing, fundraising activities, or taxing editorial and production "bubbles." To find out more, come see us at www.futurecycle.org.

THE FUTURECYCLE POETRY BOOK PRIZE

All full-length volumes of poetry published by FutureCycle Press in a given calendar year are considered for the annual FutureCycle Poetry Book Prize. This allows us to consider each submission on its own merits, outside of the context of a contest. Too, the judges see the finished book, which will have benefitted from the beautiful book design and strong editorial gloss we are famous for.

The book ranked the best in judging is announced as the prize-winner in the subsequent year. There is no fixed monetary award; instead, the winning poet receives an honorarium of 20% of the total net royalties from all poetry books and chapbooks the press sold online in the year the winning book was published. The winner is also accorded the honor of being on the panel of judges for the next year's competition; all judges receive copies of all contending books to keep for their personal library.

9 781942 371960